THIS EDITION OF COOL HUNTING; A GUIDE TO HIGH DESIGN AND INNOVATION IS
PUBLISHED BY ARRANGEMENT WITH EAST STREET PUBLICATIONS, AUSTRALIA.

FIRST PUBLISHED IN THE UK IN 2007 BY SOUTHBANK PUBLISHING,
21 GREAT ORMOND STREET, LONDON WC1N 3JB

WWW.SOUTHBANKPUBLISHING.COM

A CIP CATALOGUE RECORD FOR THIS BOOK IS AVAILABLE FROM THE BRITISH
LIBRARY.

ISBN 10: 1-904915-22-1
ISBN 13: 978-1-904915-22-5

BOOK DESIGNED BY ALEXANDER BIANCHINI-KOMETER
COVER DESIGN BY GEORGE LEWIS

FRONT COVER IMAGE - STILTS - WWW.EELKOMOORER.COM
BACK COVER IMAGE - DOGGLES - WWW.DOGGLES.COM

2 4 6 8 10 9 7 5 3 1

PRINTED AND BOUND IN CHINA BY 1010 PRINTING INTERNATIONAL

COOL /KUL/, ADJ.
NEITHER WARM NOR
VERY COLD.
NOT FRIENDLY OR
INTERESTED: A COOL
RECEPTION-V. MAKE
OR BECOME COOL

HUNT-ING CHASE
(TO KILL). SEARCH FOR.
TO PURSUE WITH INTENT
TO CAPTURE OR KILL

COOL HUNTING; TO
LOOK FOR THINGS
FROM AROUND THE
GLOBE THAT ARE
REALLY COOL

cool hunting

DAVE EVANS

southbank
publishing

www.southbankpublishing.com

indigo helmets

flowlab skateboard

geek bike

the lace fence

rocking stool

molokini

wheelsurf

hoodie

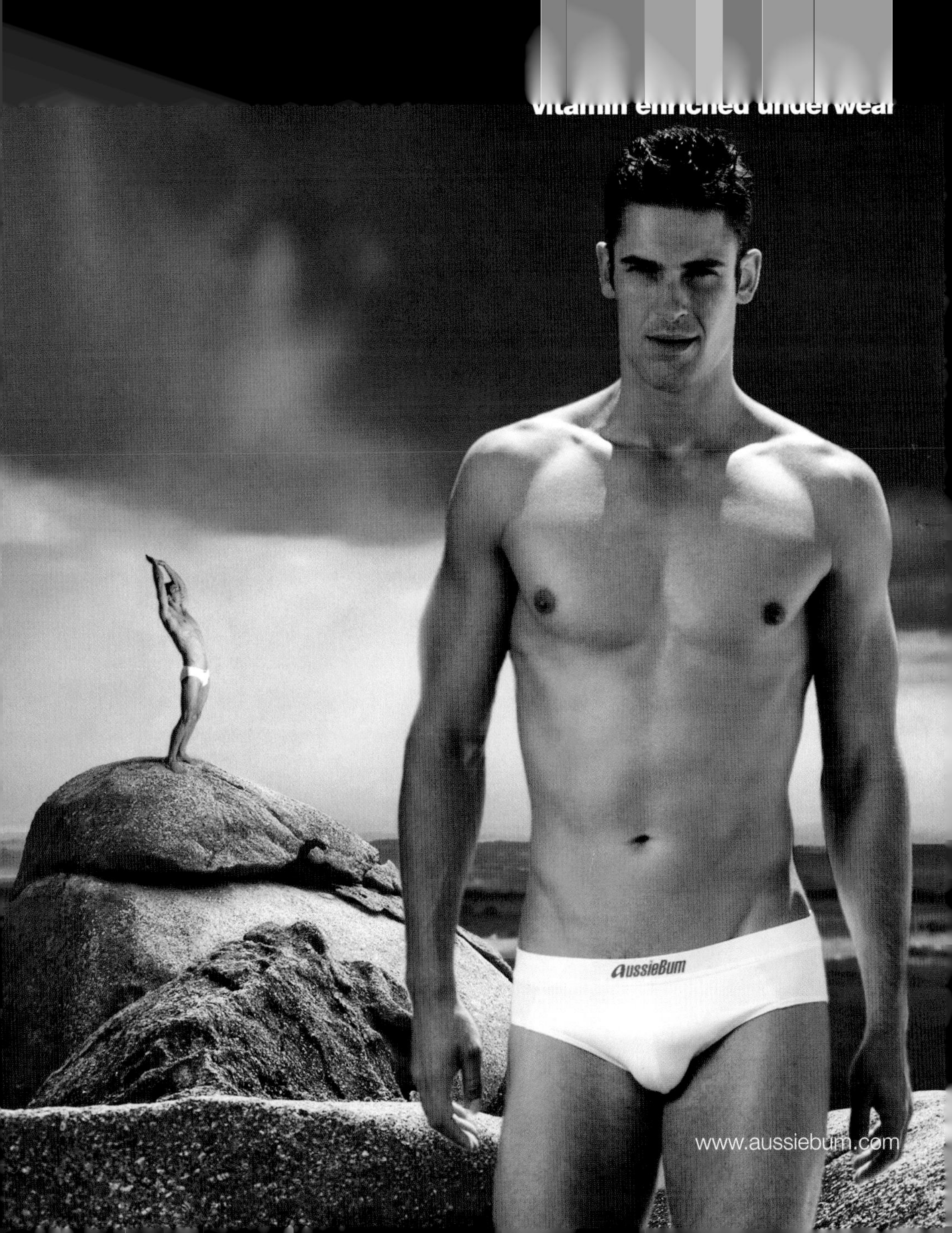
vitamin enriched underwear
aussieBum
www.aussiebum.com

t duster t-shirt recycling

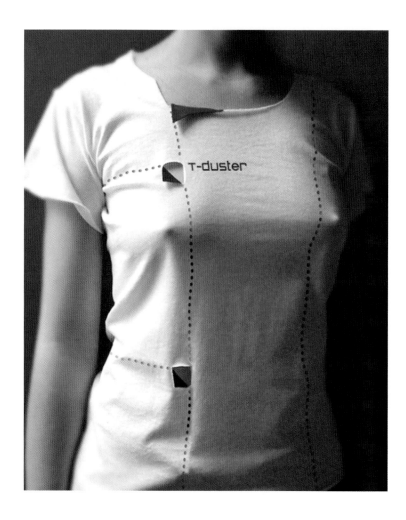

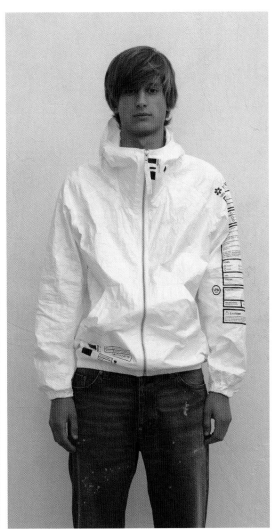

sweet november

pink uniform

www.tgclothing.com

armour corset

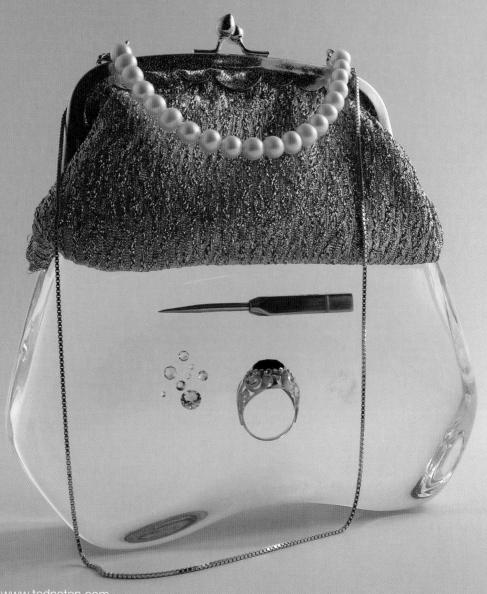

fatal attraction

www.tednoten.com

hungry jack

www.vliegervandam.com

guardian angel

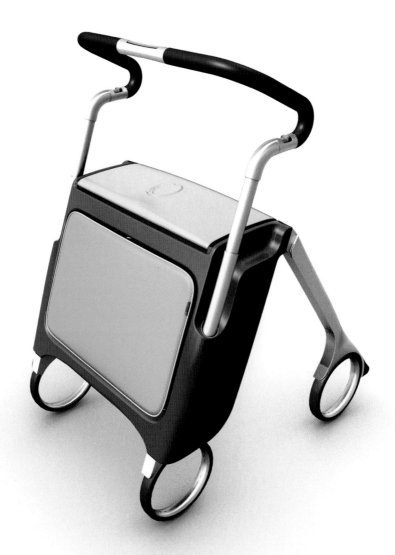

peep show

not a laptop

solar device-charging backpack

sun trap solar powered handbag

www.rosannakilfedder.com

hands-free bracelet bag

www.arzadesign.com

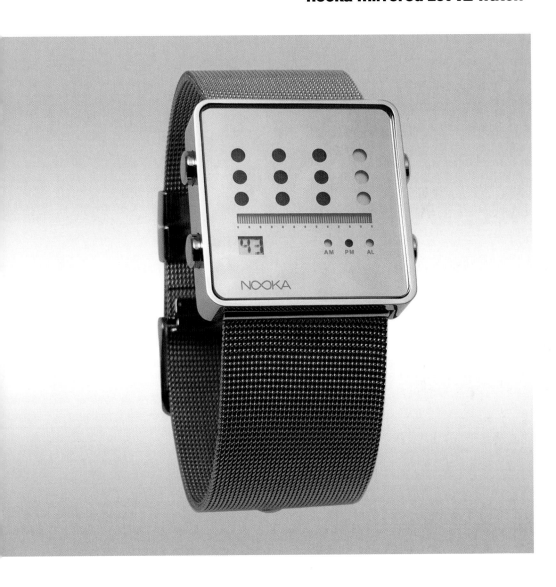

brooches from a mercedes

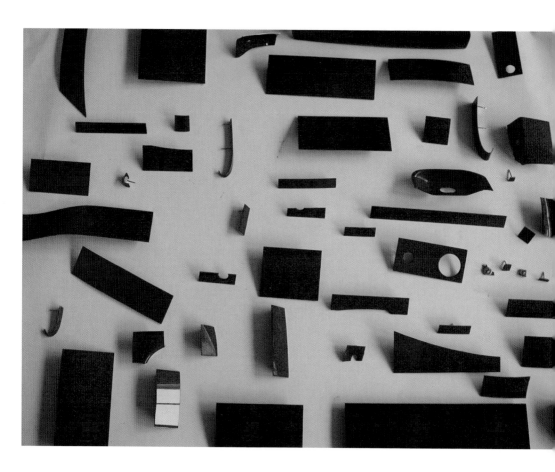

golden jubilee

phuze nauti-less ring

Instructions for use

PLAN A*

1, Fall in love

2, Get married

3, Live happy ever

*Please note:
If PLAN A fails resort to PLAN B

PLAN B

1, Cut ALL ties

www.ambrefrance.co.uk

beer/soda can ring

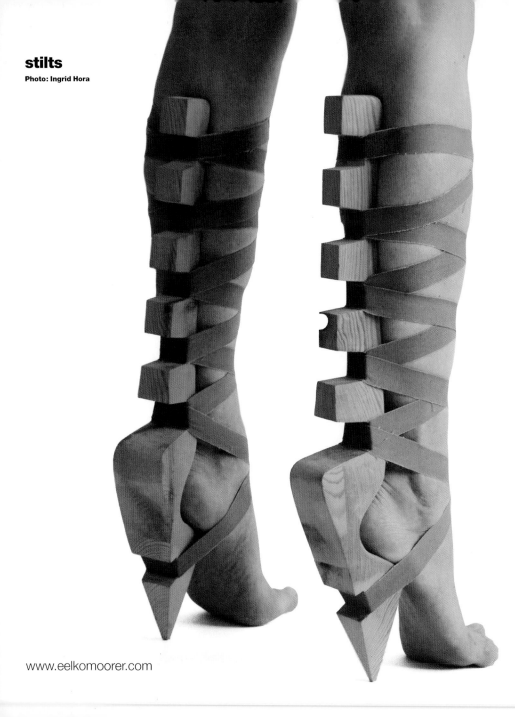

stilts

Photo: Ingrid Hora

www.eelkomoorer.com

the perfect flip flop

mija bed and dining table

doggles

chicken eglu

www.omlet.co.uk

www.evasolo.com

fish condo

AntWorks™

remote control shark

pee t-shirt and pee plush

ebola

www.giantmicrobes.com

potty

www.promisedesign.info

SUG toy

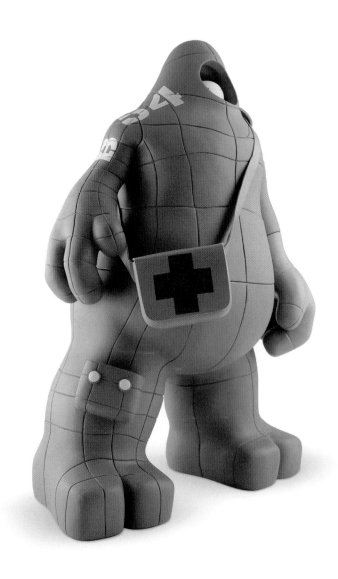

www.unklbrand.com

mr suicide bath plug

www.alessi.com

hazmapo toy

living dead dolls - arachne & mildred

stickers for the ipod shuffle

www.shufflesome.com

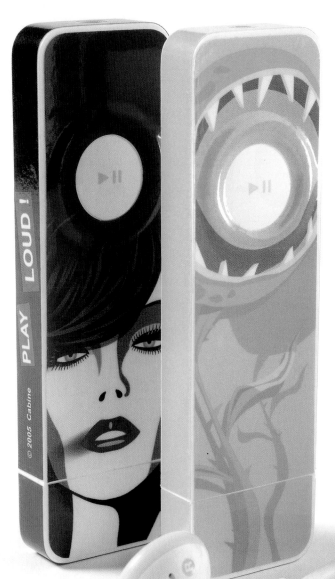

i-duck set

pe man

remote control beads

quicktionary

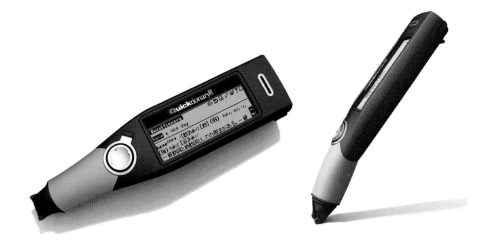

www.i2d.co.il

ambient

phonograph wine cabinet

inclosia softradio alarm clock

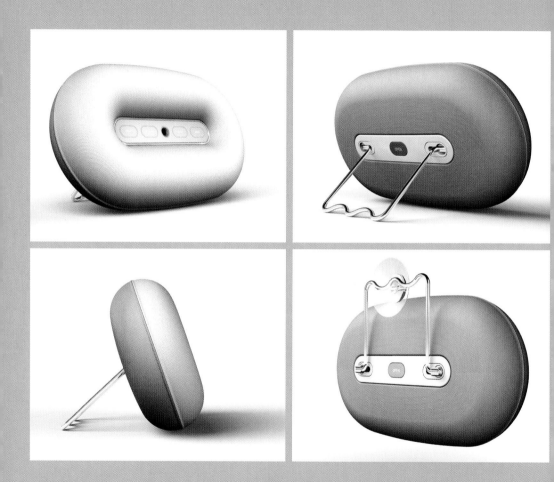

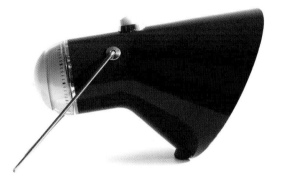

www.itaypotash.com

xrayLED wind-up torch

wattson household energy counter

www.diykyoto.com

the jimi

www.thejimi.com.au

flapart

100 dollars of confetti

hers key holder

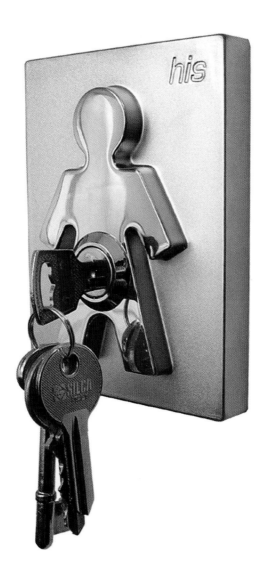

his

dressing up mirror

stiletto hooks

www.susanbradley.co.uk

salve hanger

fifi & fafa wall hangers

www.banalextra.it

inflatable pin cushion

www.clocky.net

jesus dress up

flik

www.black-blum.com

table mat

picnic cup

FOLDS FLAT

3guns vase

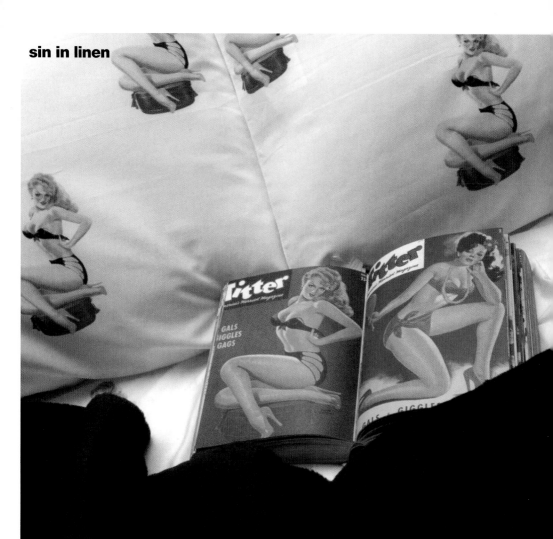

mile high kit

DNA profiling and storage kit

chocolate artistry

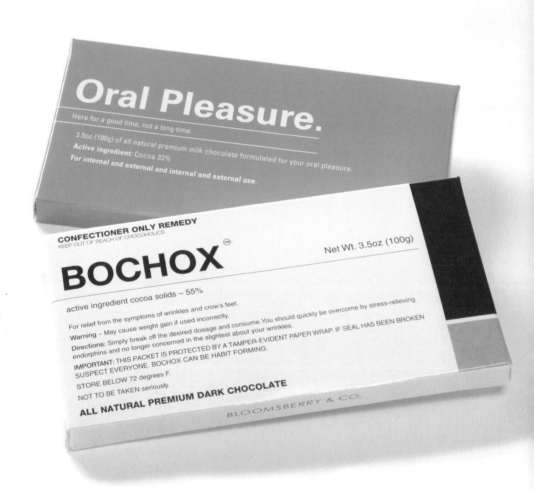

www.bloomsberry.com

iron wine

www.ironwine.com

joujou lollipop

eggling crack and grow

expanding herb pot

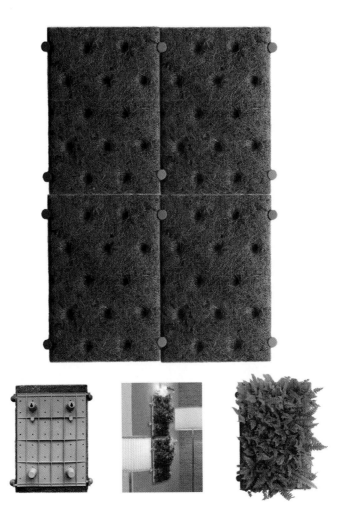

rolypig composter

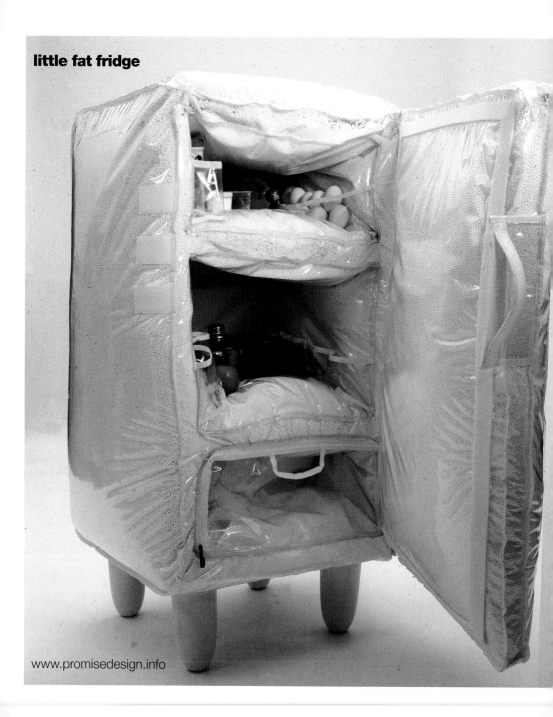

little fat fridge

electric hot plate

kitchen scales

www.evasolo.com

egg and muffin toaster

www.eggandmuffintoaster.com

selector mug

www.suck.uk.com

cognac tipping glasses

armadillo breadbin

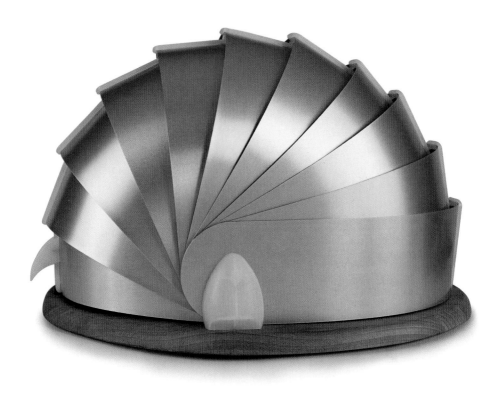

tea stick

voodoo knife holder

still life

nest

www.mozzee.co.uk

juicy boobs

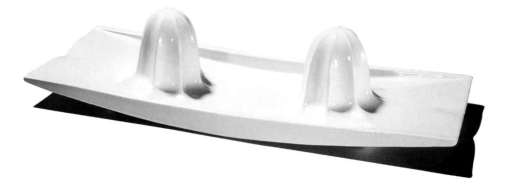

taste of talking salt & pepper

intoto float vase

handful of plates

don't ashtray

Photo: Critter Knutsen

www.joshowen.com

phonecard ashtray

vintage record bowl

'bobby' decanter

fruit bowl

www.366cm.com

laser cut flower vase

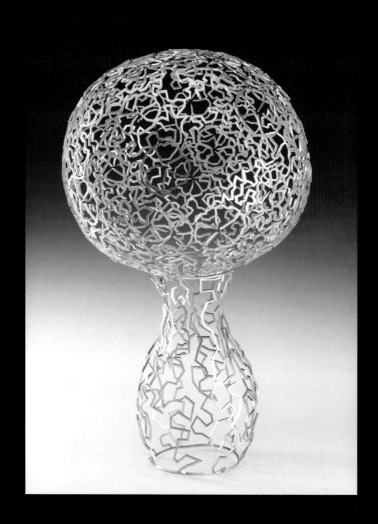

vase of phases

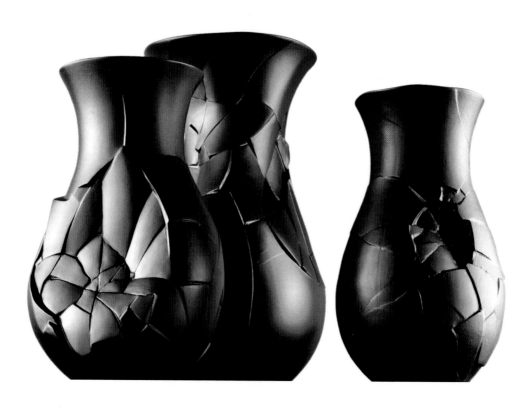

broken martini

gold plated air force 1 custom bling

the jumpers

www.janvonholleben.com

mirror carp

fashion, art, architecture, design and literature fusion

padma

Photo: Jacqui Way

www.emmahack.com.au

anatomy of a murder, by jim rosenau

magazine plant

spiral bookshelf

Photo: Maxim Saber

www.promisedesign.info

lampscape

www.roije.com

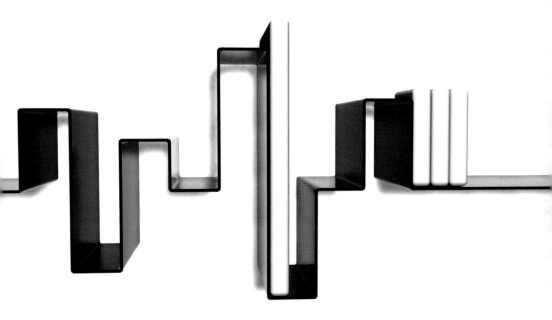

lifelight portable lamp

reading light

twisttogether lamp

natural lighting system

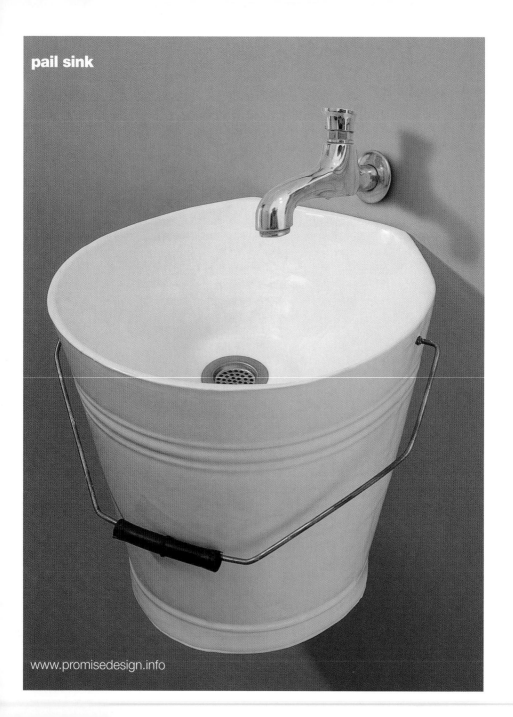

pail sink

www.promisedesign.info

moody aquarium sink

fireorb

www.fireorb.net

the rubber bearskin rug

Photo: Barend van Herpe

www.eelkomoorer.com

bahavana, carpet of polyethylene beads

bachar

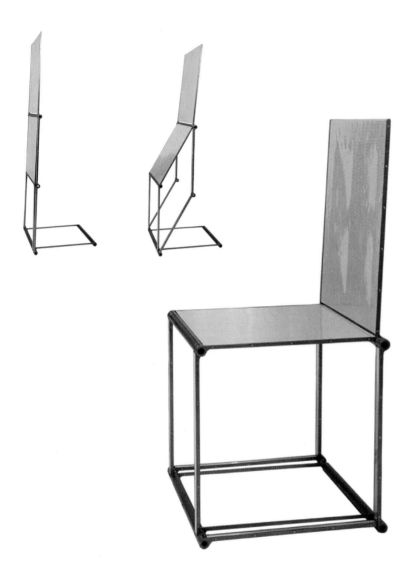

windowseat lounge

www.mikeandmaaike.com

fashion chair

annie the shopping trolley chair

re-pocket

www.promisedesign.info

5 minute chair

feel, seating system

www.molodesign.com

napshell

flirtstation

Photo: Joe Sands

www.chmoebel.com

tripple chair

bunker table & chairs
Photo: Tyl dhe Nije

www.eelkomoorer.com

pick chair

the waiting chairs

www.lwindesign.com

new Baghdad

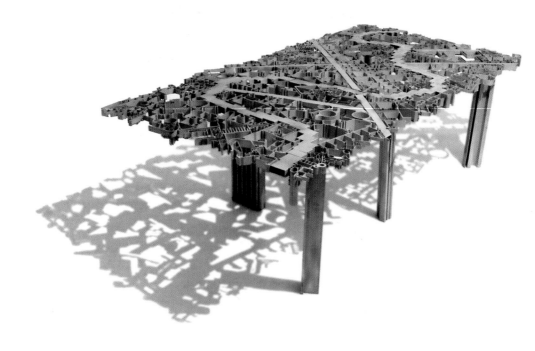

floyd

drink

www.set26.ch

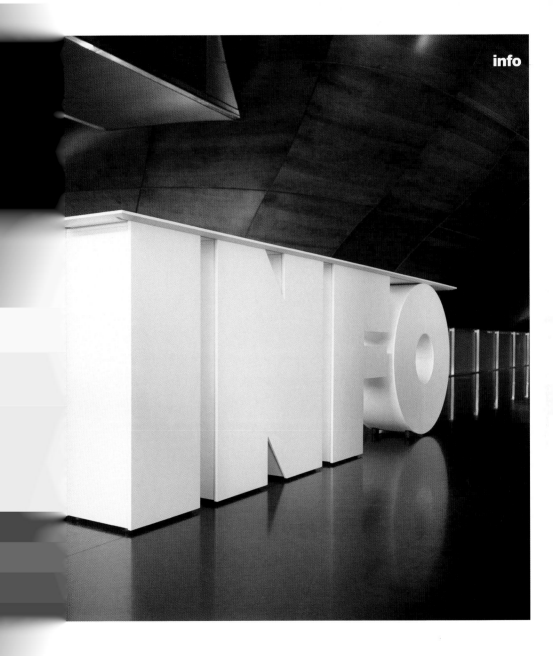

www.set26.ch

sunday papers chair

alpha

www.designkoop.com

office in a bucket

softwall

www.molodesign.com

outdoor wallpaper

compact wardrobe

wash, dry, iron

whirlpool bodybox

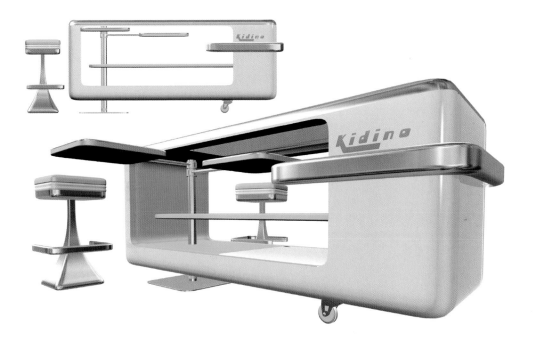

eryn

peartree treehouse

everland portable hotel

www.envbike.com

www.venturi.fr

DELIRIOUS DENIM

by ZHANG HUIGUANG & LUO LV

As the epitome of 'devil-may care' cool, denim jeans have been embraced by people from all cultures and walks of life. A global phenomenon; denim jeans have been favoured for their versatility and style.

Delirious Denim chronicles the garment's meteoric rise in popularity and its role in the building of iconic brands such as Levis and their association with icons like James Dean and Andy Warhol. This volume also showcases the creative and infinitely varied modifications of jeans in order to demonstrate the unique identity of the wearer. Insightful interviews with collectors and aficionados help articulate the irresistible allure of denim.

Fully illustrated with outstanding images, *Delirious Denim* is a colourful visual tribute to denim.

Flexi cover   210 x 145mm   400 pages with full colour illustrations

To order your copy Price £19.99 including free postage and packing (UK and Eire only); £23 for overseas orders. For credit card orders phone Turnaround Customer Services on 020 8829 3002. For orders via post – Cheques payable to Southbank Publishing, 21 Great Ormond St, London WC1N 3JB; Email to info@southbankpublishing.com

Brands A-Z: ADIDAS
by CHEN JIAOJIAO

Brands A-Z is a series that tells the story of independent, creative and alternative brands, with each title examining the history of a chosen brand, reflecting its corporate culture and showcasing its winning designs.

Brands A-Z: Adidas focuses on the definitive advertising campaigns by the brand, charts the creative thinking processes that produced the much-acclaimed campaigns over the years and showcases a series of creative artwork. Featuring interviews with designers, it explores the corporate culture of the street-wear giant providing readers with an unusual insight into the brand. This visually stunning book is a must-have for advertisers, designers and Adidas fans the world over.

Special Hardcover in Exclusive Adidas Carrier   250 x 190mm   240 pages with full colour illustrations

To order your copy Price £22.00 including free postage and packing (UK and Eire only); £25 for overseas orders. For credit card orders phone Turnaround Customer Services on 020 8829 3002. For orders via post – Cheques payable to Southbank Publishing, 21 Great Ormond St, London WC1N 3JB; Email to info@southbankpublishing.com

SNEAKERS
by ZHANG HUIGUANG & LUO LV

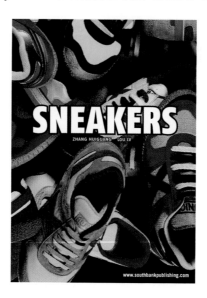

This unique book traces the evolution of sneakers from early canvas shoes to the sophisticated innovations, materials and aesthetics of the present-day sneaker. It documents sneaker culture on streets all over the world and examines how brands like Nike, Adidas, Puma, Converse, Airwalk and Vans forge distinct identities and loyalties among their fans.

Now established as an international fashion staple, the sneaker is also a versatile canvas for creative and infinitely unique customisations. This lavishly illustrated volume brings together the most original and inspired work, complemented by insightful interviews with Sneaker designers and connoisseurs.

Flexicover   210 x 145mm   400 pages with full colour illustrations

To order your copy   Price £19.99 including free postage and packing (UK and Eire only); £23 for overseas orders. For credit card orders phone Turnaround Customer Services on 020 8829 3002. For orders via post – Cheques payable to Southbank Publishing, 21 Great Ormond St, London WC1N 3JB; Email to info@southbankpublishing.com

DESIGNERS LEAGUE
by DAVID POLICOFF

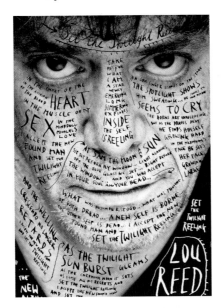

In *Designers League* the work of contemporary design luminaries from around the world is brought together in one stunning volume. Included are cutting-edge examples of packaging design and Word Art, corporate and logo design, print design and orientation systems.

This sumptuous volume provides a tour of some of the most exciting innovators in their field today, giving a valuable insight into the way they work, think and achieve their success. It is a must-have for designers, cultural historians and all those interested in the way excellence is achieved in the field of the creative arts.

Hardback   290 x 230mm   418 pages with full colour illustrations

To order your copy Price £30.00 including free postage and packing (UK and Eire only); £33 for overseas orders. For credit card orders phone Turnaround Customer Services on 020 8829 3002. For orders via post – Cheques payable to Southbank Publishing, 21 Great Ormond St, London WC1N 3JB; Email to info@southbankpublishing.com